99 Fabulous
Food Websites
You Can't Eat Without

Plus

The Seven Course Finale

by Jim and Peter Spellos

99 Food Logo Image: Mark LaRiviere
Cover and Book Design: KN Design
Proofreading: Marjorie Messinger

ISBN: 978-0-6151-3612-7

Published by Lulu.com

To our Mom, Diana Spellos…

Who taught us everything we needed to learn…
and a whole lot more.

Today's Menu

Recipes

Hungry & Thirsty

Educational & Reference

Goulash

If you can catch a chef in a quiet, reflective moment over a drink, and ask what the worst aspects of the job are, you will probably get the following answer: "The heat, the pressure, the fast pace, the isolation from normal society, the long hours, the pain, the relentless, never-ending demands of the profession."

If you wait awhile, maybe two more drinks, and ask again - this time inquiring about the best parts of being a chef - more often than not, the chef will pause, take another sip of beer, smile...and give you exactly the same answer.

- Anthony Bourdain

Preface
(Spellos the Younger)

The older I get, the more I can't remember. Did I close the garage door? Return all my phone calls? Put the dog out (wait – we don't even have a dog). But ask me about the time Peter and I had dinner at The French Laundry, and my memory crystallizes. Seeing that first course Thomas Keller brought out (Oysters and Pearls) still resonates deep inside. Food has that effect, doesn't it?

Food can define moments in time. Recall images that we've long forgotten (or so we thought). Bring a smile to our face, just from an aroma that reminds us of our childhood.

As I've traveled around the United States & Canada for the past 25 years, first running conferences, now teaching WAY COOL technology tools, food has been a way to connect with hundreds of friends and colleagues. Meals shared (and sometimes enjoyed alone) frequently made those long days worthwhile.

But even before that, food had an enormous impact on me (even though, if you ask my Mom, she'll tell you I was a very picky eater – she still can't believe I finish all my vegetables). As a kid, I remember watching PBS. When some kids were watching Sesame Street, I was enjoying The Galloping Gourmet and Julia Child. Cooking shows were more than just a way to pass the day. They were exposing me to foods I could only dream about tasting.

Then there were the Sunday afternoon's with the family. The shame of that all is that I was far too young to appreciate what it all meant. In retrospect, while I may have thought that it was the Pastitsio that made the day tolerable, it really was being with family that made the food taste so good.

The idea for 99 Fabulous Food Websites, then, was pretty much a no-brainer. Take the things I'm passionate about (teaching, technology and food) and bring them all together. However, one small catch. Something was missing in the equation, as I knew the book should be written, but I just wasn't getting around to it.

When Peter and I then started talking about working together, it all made perfect sense. We both shared the passion about food, as well as sharing the love for one another. As we get older, it just makes sense to work more with people you care about. We started comparing notes and information, and jeesh, it just came together like a great meal does.

Since this is a preface, the requisite thank yous are in order, and plenty of folks have had a huge impact on my life (or, as Yogi would say, "I'd like to thank all of the people who made my life necessary.") But let's cut it down to three. Peter - who else made it their goal at dinnertime to see if food could actually come out my nose? Mom, I really was listening and absorbing everything you said (I just never wanted to admit it as a kid). And to my wife, Marjorie…it just wouldn't be worth a thing without you.

So, dig in and enjoy the food websites. There's plenty of room for seconds, too!

Jim

Preface
(Spellos the Older)

I'm the luckiest man on earth. No really. I'm 52 years old, and doing what I was doing when I was 16. Entertaining, creating, performing and coaching, I've done what I only dreamed of as a teenager. I'm an actor/comedian/denture wearer. Sure, when I was in high school, I thought life would look much different than it does now. You know, lifetime achievement awards, mass adoration, a sandwich named after me at Carnegie Deli!!! In reality, life wound up not like that at all, though the folks at Carnegie always comply with more ham for this ham upon request. Extra meat charge, naturally. My life is simple. I love that I still get to play and create for a living – over 100 film and TV appearances, comedy shows around the country, voice-overs and my passion for the last 25 years, teaching and coaching my younger, more agile and much loved peers.

Having truly done with my life what I set out to do, I was at a sweet impasse, a place for the 1st time in my life where, I had no goals, no vistas. I'd done what I'd said I'd do. I didn't want to ever stop acting or performing, it wasn't that at all. I just didn't have to prove anything anymore, to me or the world. Not that there wasn't anything in life I was interested in pursuing. Don't get me wrong, this was a great place to be at in one's life. The options abound, yet the question stood silent. What do I *want* to do? Life goes on whether I stand to view it or dive in and swim in any direction. And now, at 52, I felt I had accomplished and became who I wanted to become. I was, and still am, an actor. You know. *That* guy. You know, not the big star, but *that guy*? You know, he was in that *show?* I spent my life, my career in essence, playing intimately with strangers. So, who do you want to play with now?

My brother, period. My favorite human being ever. My answer was clear and simple. When I left NYC for LA in 1989, I left everything I ever knew and went in search of all I didn't know, all that I wanted to become. Now, realizing the dream was just living the life, and that we accomplish all we truly want, by being who we truly are. I knew who I was. Spent plenty of money on therapies, drugs and seminars to shed some light in that area, I garon-tee! What was missing was time with my younger brother again. Hell, I sneezed and 17 years in California went by in a David Crosby-like flashback. My BABY brother was 47, married for 20 years to his love Marjorie. Our mom Diana is now 85, and 7 years cancer-free. The days were endless, but life was flying by. I missed them all, dearly. As Messers. Newly and Bricusse once wrote, "Stop the World, I Want to Get Off."

So I did. Alas, I always did what I wanted to do rather than what I should do. (much to the chagrin of family, ex-friends and the former Mrs. Spellos – but that's another book) and it was time to do it again. I told Kim (family nickname – another book) that I wanted us to spend more time together. I suggested that somehow my 35 years of entertaining (or annoying) the public could perhaps help him in his profession. He's also a great teacher in his own right. See, we both had become coaches and mentors along the way to living out all the passions of our lives, he in the technology field, me in the arts. Teaching people about simplicity. Teaching people about choice. Teaching ourselves again and again to play and live with abandon.

Thus began many conversations we had about life, the quality of it, and the amount of time we'd rather spend on the things we love, with those we love. Make time for what you want, don't be a slave to what you think you need to do. Simple in theory, not always easy to execute. Still, follow your heart and you'll get to where you need to be. We decided we need to be together more. So, why not write about what we love? Sports? Technology? Comedy? So much food for thought....say, what about food? In our 20's we watched the Playboy Channel, in our 30's, it was ESPN, now waxing and waning at 50, The Food Network is our only must see TV. We love to cook, we love to eat and we love to talk about cooking and eating. The sails were set to serve the seven courses! Or some botched food/oceanic metaphor like that....

Preface

Since we've written our first book on the subject of food and where to indulge said food habits on the Internet, it obviously has a purpose and a passion in our lives. Jim has spent much time in the hospitality industry and traveling. I have spent many après show hours eating great late nights at the diners of the America with my creative inmates. Collectively, we are a quarter ton of fun, laughter and gratitude. Life has treated us well and we love our lives and hobbies. We knew this passion of ours was something we longed to write about, then shout it out to our fellow food fanatics out there. (After all, we are grandsons of a former Greek diner owner that still stands on 9th Avenue in NYC.) So, what does this all mean, aside from the fact that we can wash a mean dish?

It means we are brothers, with a great love for each other, with some time left on our hands to play together again, although that damn timer in the kitchen keeps ticking faster and faster. We are not culinary authorities. We are not food experts. We are more like a couple of baby boomer bears who still think they're bear cubs. Eating, frolicking, hibernating…..Listen, if you're not doing what you love, with the people you love, as often as you wish, then what in the wide, wide world of sports are you doing with your life ??!?!

That brings us to why *this* book to start our series of 99's. This is our chance to bring to the table a ready-to-eat food reference fun book. It is our amuse bouche dedicated to the amazing folks who have touched our lives, fed us literally and spiritually, and to all those that we have not broken bread with yet. The recipe for this book, nay for The Fabulous Spellos Brothers, is simple. Combine a two big handfuls of who we are with a pound of what we love, fold gently and serve up 99 reasons to make sure you have a never-ending family-style table feast of food facts and fun. Our book is our toast to you. Until next we meet or eat, some closing thoughts. In case I never do get to the Oscar's, I thank: my parents for staying together long enough to make sure my brother appeared, then stayed in this world; my mother for her steadfast belief and unwavering support, my father for his love of port and Papaya King; Kim for his love of me; Bunny for her love of Cubby; Jim Brownold for his brilliance and his t-t-timing; Roselyne for her chicken, Baltimore and her courage; Brigitte, my former, whose key unlocked the floodgates; Kelly for daring to dream; Sharma for helping me clear the mirror; Jennifer Lehman for making me be naked; Jim Wynorksi and Fred Ray for Orville Ketchum and G. Gordon Baer; Laura Adler for making my AMERICAN DREAMS come true; all who I have shared the stage, my true home and heart's blood; those who've laughed at the same stories a dozen times and to the few left who still do; and to that fat kid who never, ever, ever, ever stopped believing.

P.Spellos, esq., xxl
10/27/06

Forward

First and foremost, this is a guide book focused on giving food lovers and home chefs everywhere 99 great culinary resources. Whether you cook for fun, for your family or for a living, we hope these websites offer valuable, information, services, knowledge and humor on a myriad of culinary topics and fields, from Asian Cuisine to Zagats to Go!

Recipes is what the culinary world craves the most, and we made sure you got a pantry full, not only in our RECIPES chapter, but throughout all the other chapters. There are so many wonderful websites we encountered that didn't make our first 99's List. We've added many of those links all through the book, as our "lagniappe" to you.

We wanted to make this a book you could linger over with a latte and enjoy, or search for that special ingredient you needed at the last minute. Check out the INDEX in the back for a quick way to find things you want and things you might not know you need. Then search for your favorite chef, cooking school or hard-to-find spice!

However you choose to read or use our guide, we thank you for helping us spread the love of food and hope our offering can enhance all those who feed our bodies, hearts and minds. The enjoyment of a meal together, the history of its origins or the simple task of preparation can bring together so many of us who are worlds apart that we would never encounter elsewhere. We are honored to be a part of this community.

We encourage you to contact us with your favorite recipe, what you liked about this book (or even didn't) a WAY COOL food-related story or your list for The Seven Course Finale!

Forward

Please check out our website at www.the99s.com, our blog at http://fabulousspellosbrothers.typepad.com, or contact us via e-mail, at either peterspellos@gmail.com or jspellos@meeting-u.com.

Well, it's almost time for our feeding, so thanks for being a part of our lives and our first book! Opa!

The Fabulous Spellos Brothers
Jim and Peter Spellos
10/30/06

Recipes

IN THE BEGINNING....

The Food Network
the cooking wheel, re-invented
www.foodnetwork.com

Well, to be exact, 1993. That is when the TV Food Network, as it was known back then, came into our lives, and changed the way Americans ate. They also understood the way we got our information was changing as well. The Information Superhighway united a hungry culinary consumer community and made stars and celebrities of local chefs and far away "fat ladies." It was a Brave New and Tasty World, and they brought to the table not only entertainment, but a way to reconnect with our own families, as well as those around the world. They reminded us of the one simple thing we all did everyday. Eat.

Their website today would take days to inform you about and we'd never ever come even close to sharing all the WAY COOL things on their site. Recipes, Videos, massive recipes database from ALL their shows, Shop Food TV, it is joyously infinite. Hey, are *you* the next Food TV Star?

CHEFS

THE ESSENCE OF FOOD ON TV

Chef Emeril Lagasse
fall river's favorite son
www.emerils.com

If Julia Child was the Queen of the TV Kitchens, then most certainly Chef Emeril Lagasse is its' Crown (and Clown) Prince. His place in the pantheon of celebrity chefs is both undeniable and unmistakable. First, he completely demystified "gourmet" cooking for the masses. He took white linen dining and taught us to make it in white Formica kitchens. He turned said kitchen from a domain of dutiful domesticity, into the family centerpiece for fun and food, where if you follow some directions, good fun and good food can nourish far more than the human body. Secondly, his live studio audience long-running show, Emeril Live! catapulted The Food Network to the immense popularity and still growing audience it has today. Each and every recognizable master chef and celebrity food meister of today owes a huge debt of thanks to Chef Lagasse, whose BAM! exploded the world of food on television to "notches unknown to man!!!!

Emeril's website is as fun and flashy as the Pork Fat Ruler himself! Restaurants is where you can make reservations at any of his nine restaurants nationwide, whether its' dinner for two or a planned party. We had the pleasure of celebrating Peter's 50th birthday at Delmonico's in Las Vegas with 16 close friends. The top notch food and first rate service is not to be missed. Neither is the impressive wine cellar.

Go to the Cooking section of the website and find Emeril's Notes from the Kitchen, devoted to getting you information on Culinary History, Food Finds, Kitchen Tips and more. His Shop page is beautifully photographed, giving you hundreds of options on Emeril's cookware and tableware. Food Of Love highlights his brands of seasonings, salsas and sauces.

The worlds of food and technology just got tastier. Download Emeril's Meals2Go or Recipes2Go to your website, and take the Chef to the grocery store next time you need a new idea for dinner or any occasion. We cannot forget his vast and delicious database of recipes. Just type in an ingredient and you're off to the kitchen.

We chose to talk more about Emeril Lagasse, not only because of how his love of food and "food of love" inspired our own, but because of his charitable efforts (like The Emeril Lagasse Foundation – www.emeril.org) where he lends his name, heart and soul. Now more than ever, we could all use some of that "essence" in our everyday lives. Thanks, Chef!

LOVE, ITALIAN STYLE

Mario Batali
minister of italian cuisine, orange clogs aficionado
www.mariobatali.com

You won't find our Ambassador to Italy at the embassy, nor at the United Nations. You will usually find him tending one of his world-renowned restaurants, or most assuredly on your TV screen. Of course we are talking about Chef Mario Batali, the playful, passionate Iron Chef, restaurateur, and cookbook author. His larger-than-life personality has helped bring not just the flavors of Italy to our tables, but the rich food history of that country as well.

Mario's site (highlighted in orange like his clogs) is much like the amazing dishes we've had the pleasure of sampling at his fine restaurants: simple, fresh ingredients cooked and served to perfection. Click on Recipes and start cooking! The Restaurant and Cookbooks section has thumbnails of all his 7 culinary venues, plus his Italian Wine Merchants.

HALLES RAISER

Anthony Bourdain
culinary sherpa – "a cook's tour" of duty
www.anthonybourdain.com

Shakespeare said, "the play's the thing." With chef/author/CBGB's fan Anthony Bourdain, it's more like "the plate's the thing." Whatever's on that plate, he'll try it. What we dig about him is he's the Howard Cosell of the kitchen. He tells it like it is. Whether in his books or on the fantastic No Reservations on The Travel Channel, you come away feeling it would be as much fun chowing down with him as it would eating his creations at Les Halles in Manhattan.

Bourdain's website is smart, sharp, and to the point, like its' chef. You can buy his novels or cookbooks, get a great Les Halles recipe or read interviews. If you like your food or your opinions on the bland side, Bourdain is not for you. But if it's life's spice or the spice of life that you crave, then the nasty boy of *The Nasty Bits* is number one on our charts with a bullet, or boulette, if we're lucky.

FRONTERA AND CENTER

Chef Rick Bayless
maestro of gourmet mexican cuisine
www.fronterakitchens.com

Chef Rick Bayless is another of the great renaissance men of the 21st century kitchen. Chef/author/teacher, his authentic Mexican cuisine has garnished him with numerous James Beard awards, but combining good food and healthy eating seem to be his greatest reward and joy. Check out his website with his restaurants or recipes and you'll read rave upon rave. The site is entertaining and colorful. In 1994, Frontera Grill was selected the worlds' third most casual restaurant!

Check out Rick's Cooking And Entertaining ideas. See what's in Rick's Pantry and try out new cooking techniques (the tequila-infused Queso Fundido sounds perfect). If you don't know him, take the time and lose your hunger to Mexico- One Plate at a Time with Rick Bayless on TV. Ole!

BUTTER ME UP

Paula Dean
celebrity chef, down-home delight
www.ladyandsons.com

If down home is your home, if you love comfort food served with a heapin' helpin' of luv, if you love butter, you love Paula Dean (and who doesn't!). "The Bag Lady" herself is one of the hottest (and coolest) celebrity chefs on the scene today. If you don't know her story, then you don't know half the reasons to love her. If you've eaten at The Lady and Sons or tried her recipes, then you already know the other half.

Paula's site covers everything Paula, from the restaurant and its' banquet facilities to Paula's Cooking School, where you'll learn from The Lady herself. Of course, you can purchase her great cookbooks, spices, accessories and more. Link on over to (her brother) Uncle Bubba's Oyster house. You may never eat north of the Mason-Dixon line again!

THE MAGIC OF K-PAUL

Chef Paul Prudhomme
louisiana culinary legend
www.chefpaul.com

Any conversation about Cajun/Creole cooking must include the great Chef Paul. His larger-than-life joy for cooking matches well with his line of Magic Seasoning Blends, which has taken the taste of his Louisiana kitchen worldwide. Chef shares many of his delicious recipes on his site, and once tried you can order his cookbooks or DVD's for more fun.

A dedicated page to K-Paul's Louisiana Kitchen is yours to enjoy, peeking at a menu that'll make you call up your travel agent immediately. Then go to the Videos page, and watch Chef Paul as he takes you step-by-step through some of his favorite recipes. Spice up your world with Chef Paul.

EMPEROR OF THE SUN-DRIED TOMATOES

Chef Wolfgang Puck
live, love, eat!
www.wolfgangpuck.com

That three-word mantra is known around the world, as is his extensive food empire. Chef Wolfgang Puck is the 2nd hardest working man in show business (next to James Brown), not to mention the restaurant business. He has a string of restaurants (six in Tokyo), caters the annual Academy Awards Party Bash, can be seen playing himself on TV shows both fictional (Frazier) and reality (on Home Shopping Network). This renowned entrepreneur has combined California and French cuisines into a fun fusion, loved by millions in his eateries and at the grocery store.

The site is as bold as the chef himself. Great photos accompany his recipes, with tips from the chef. At some California grocery stores, you can snack on a fresh slice of pizza from Wolfgang while shopping the aisles for his take-home line. So, Live! Love! Click!

FROM PEA PODS TO IPODS

Chef Ming Tsai
tradition, fusion tossed with technology
www.ming.com

Chef Ming Tsai is another one of the most popular celebrity chefs around. His East-West cuisine is known to fans around the world. In the last 8 years, he's hosted three different food programs, with his current incarnation being Simply Ming, now in its third season on PBS. His restaurant Blue Ginger has been wowing patrons since 1998. He is the national spokesperson for the Food Allergy and Anaphylaxis Network.

Chef Tsai gets a WAY COOL nod from us for using technology to further reach out to his hungry audience. Just go to iTunes and type "Simply Ming" into the search box. Then download his weekly podcasts and take Ming Tsai and his great cooking and technique tips with you to any kitchen you want!

MICHELIN MAN

Chef Thomas Keller
the french laundry
www.frenchlaundry.com

Reservations are accepted *two months* in advance for Chef Thomas Keller's The French Laundry in Yountville, CA, so put down this book (only for a minute, though) and call now. Then spend the next 60 days dreaming about what you might have to eat if you had but one meal to eat. Don't waste your time. Chef Keller has you covered. The first and only American-born chef to have two, three-star restaurants since the Michelin guides inception in 1900. We'll say that again. Since 1900.

Chef Keller's other restaurants include Bouchon, Bouchon Las Vegas, and in 2004 he opened Per Se in New York City. He truly is a one-of-a-kind culinary artisan. He creates the most memorable meals combining his passions with his dedication to cook with the freshest seasonal ingredients. Two months is well worth the wait, we promise. And if you can't go, call us, we will!!!

CRAFTING A RECIPE FOR SUCCESS

Chef Tom Colicchio
restaurateur, top chef
www.craftrestaurant.com

New York City is a big city with a big appetite. Nobody serves The Big Apple better than Chef Tom Colicchio, with his fine and fun cuisine. Since 1994 when he opened Gramercy Tavern, he has been wowing both the critics and the New Yawkahs alike. In 2002, his Craft Restaurant was selected Best New Restaurant nationwide, by the prestigious James Beard Foundation. His food is bold, flavorful and simply prepared.

Craft Newsletter, only available on his site, is a terrific way to catch up on all the culinary events at his restaurants. Also on the fun side is 'wichcraft, both in NYC and Las Vegas, alongside their sister eatery Craftsteak. 'wichcraft serves up great cheap eats, while not skimping on terrific ingredients and careful execution that is a trademark of the chef's creations. Craft Dallas is another shining plate in the Colicchio pantry. Take a delicious bite of the apple, courtesy TCx2 – "Top Chef" Tom Colicchio.

AUTHORS

ANY FRIEND OF DEAN & DELUCA'S...

David Rosengarten
foods and wines that make me swoon
www.davidrosengarten.com

In the early days of The Food Network, David was a fixture. His minimalist kitchen set, whimsy, and love of food made him one of the networks' first recognizable faces, where he did over 2500 shows. He is a food author (*Dean and DeLuca Cookbook*, *Taste*) and authority, travel writer and TV journalist, and has served as the only American judge on an international panel that selected the world's greatest sommelier.

Rosengarten's site is sharp and easy to navigate. You can sign up for his Tastings E-Zine or his newsletter, *The Rosengarten Report*, buy his newest book *It's ALL American Food*, or even get free coupons from David's favorite foodie stores.

THE SCHWARTZ WHO ATE NEW YORK!

Arthur Schwartz
the food maven
www.foodmaven.com

As his website states, a Maven is a Yiddish word meaning connoisseur. Arthur Schwartz is just that. He was one of the first male newspaper food editors in the country, and now is a cooking instructor at major cooking schools in NYC. He is also an author, and host of The Food Maven nationally syndicated radio show.

Arthur obviously has a love affair with Italy, marked by links Restaurant Guide to Italy, Seliano Culinary Vacations and Italian Travel Links. He is truly a food lover and it shows on every page of the site. Check out his recipes from his books or radio shows, find out where he is appearing live or read his lively blog, The Maven's Diary.

SMOKE GETS IN YOUR THIGHS

Steve Raichlen
share the exception
www.barbecuebible.com

There are so many great barbecue sites (and pits) out there, but if you need schoolin' on smokin', look no further than Steve Raichlen – award-winning author, cooking instructor and the TV host of PBS' BBQ University. Steve "steaked" a claim in the pantheons of BBQ with *The Barbecue Bible*, a chronicle of his 4 year, 200,000 mile study of global grilling.

As you'd expect, there are great recipes on this site, as well as a BBQ Board, Store, and Newsletter. But don't miss the Techniques archive, because class is in session. And don't forget the corn on the cob!

MEATLESS IN SEATTLE

Anna Thomas
the vegetarian epicure
www.vegetarianepicure.com

While a grad student at UCLA, Anna Thomas wrote *The Vegetarian Epicure* and brought gourmet recipes to the vegetarian world. The *Los Angeles Times* called her cookbook, "The bible of vegetarians in the 1970's." Thomas was not satisfied in just that arena. She co-wrote and produced (with husband Gregory Nava directing) the critically acclaimed film El Norte, which was nominated for an Academy Award.

Anna continued to write screenplays (Mi Familia) and wrote *The New Vegetarian Epicure* in 1996. Her site is simple and elegant, with new recipes that you can sample from her books.

THE MUCKY UNDERBELLY OF FOOD

The Gastronaut
food adventures for the romantic,
the foolhardy and the brave
www.thegastronaut.com

The Gastronaut is the companion website to the book of the same name, taking us on an extreme culinary journey, through bizarre experiences, arcane information and appetite for new tastes and adventures. Stefan Gates calls his book "a manual for culinary show-offs." There are opportunities to sample this funny and out there (and right on) book on the website.

And speaking of sampling, Gates (who is from Great Britain) shares with us some unique recipes. There is a Bum Sandwich recipe which must be read, if not tried (with someone you like). Hopefully you'll never look at a pressed sandwich the same way again. By the time this book is published, his new BBC series, Cooking in the Danger Zone, should be on the air.

ALL THE WORLD'S A PLATE...

Mark Bittman
how to cook everything
www.howtocookeverything.tv

We could have put Mark Bittman's site anywhere in the book; recipes, reference, hungry, etc. He is a best-selling author, creator of the popular *New York Times* weekly column "The Minimalist" and most recently appeared in a 13-part series for PBS called Bittman Takes On America's Chefs.

There are terrific clips from the aforementioned series on the site, as well as many fabulous recipes from his myriad of fine cookbooks. Got a hankering for Grilled Pork Confit? (and who doesn't!) Running out of Persimmon Pudding? (and why would you?) Need another reason to click on his site?

BLOGS

SMARTER THAN THE AVERAGE BLOG

The Accidental Hedonist
kate hopkins' informative, witty, sharp food blog
www.accidentalhedonist.com

Remember when your mom told you she didn't play favorites? She lied. This is one of our favorite sites. Fun, funny, informative, easy on the eyes…sort of like Katie Couric! AH is also a portal to other food blogs, with a slant to the Seattle culinary scene.

The favorite ongoing list is her High Fructose Corn Syrup Product List. You're not gonna like what's in your favorite snacks. Check out Kate's Laws as well. Our fave? Kate's Law (not Couric's) of the Proportional Cost of Burritos – "The more money spent on a burrito, the higher probability of disappointment in the dish." Kate Hopkins and her site do not disappoint.

BLOG ON, GARTH

Chef's Blogs
culinary blogs of those in the food industry
www.chefsblogs.com

Like a simple meal at a fine restaurant, there are no frills at this food industry driven site. Just easy to browse blogs, with links to over 1000 sites by working chefs, industry staff and students, categorized by Topic, Region and more. CB also has links to blogs in over 12 foreign languages. Oui, oui!

There is also a Professional Blogs section, with a wonderful cross-section of info and opinions on subjects like culinary schools, culinary travel, industry authors, food journals, suppliers and restaurants. Blog on, Wayne.

IT'S A BIRD, IT'S A PLANE, IT'S...

Super Chef Blog
follow the careers, empires, trends of the super chefs
www.superchefblog.com

A daily homage/home page to the culinary giants of today. More business info than food info, with a decided slant to exploring the media circus that is encompassing the food world. This is a who's who portal of the hot chefs, trends and issues of the day.

Many links are to articles, but there are as many links to opportunities to purchase your favorite's chef's wares on Amazon.com. Commerce and branding rule over recipes and hints at SCB. All of the articles are thorough and intelligent, with loads of information and links. So, up, up and away to the kitchen and the world of the "super chefs."

EATING OUT

FOOD 411

Chowhound
for those who live to eat
www.chowhound.com

Now don't you be calling a chowhound, a foodie. That's like calling Trekkers, Trekkies on this wildly popular web community. Chowhounds are trailblazers, boldly going where the common mouths fear to taste. Chowhound's members are from all over the world, sharing tips, secrets and opinions on a mélange of culinary topics.

There are local "boards" across the country, with over twenty international ones, as well. They are all moderated and have special etiquette reminders before you post. On-going moderated topics include Home Cooking, Food Media and News, and Cookware. If its taste, talk and tips from food fanatics who love and live to eat, Chowhound is the place to be.

FREQUENT FRYER POINTS

Open Table
on-line reservations to fine dining
www.opentable.com

Seating over one million hungry diners per month, Open Table is one of the most popular of the on-line restaurant reservations services there is today. They have a great Dining Rewards program. Each time you dine with an OT reservation, you amass points redeemable for Dining Cheques. Once you amass enough points, you can use them with your next Open Table booked reservation.

Forty-five states have restaurants enrolled in Open Table, as well as great overseas eateries in the U.K., Japan, Canada and Mexico. When you select your home city, they offer many categories from dining al fresco to places that cater to groups.

A TABLE FOR TWO IN ANY CORNER OF THE WORLD

Restaurant Row
restaurant reservations and food services
www.restaurantrow.com

The Yellow Pages never tasted this good. Restaurant Row operates one of the largest "to go" restaurant services and information sites on the web. They have over 170,000 restaurants in over 13,000 cities and towns worldwide. Both restaurant owner and patron can list their favorite eateries info and help add to this web community. They offer simple or advanced searches to help you find the right place.

Their AvantGo.com gives all the info on Restaurant Row in the Palm (or other mobile devices) of your hand. Connoisseur Corner brings you exclusively written food articles and news. RR's newsletter alerts you to new listings in your area via e-mail.

SURVEY SAYS... ZAGAT

Zagat Survey
restaurants, nightlife, ratings & reviews
www.zagat.com

Oh, the little red and extremely read book! The Zagat Survey is the most popular consumer survey-based dining & travel guide, with over 250,000 voters participating from all over the globe. A Restaurants Only subscription to the website gives you all the great info you expect from their book, plus the ability to customize your searches, so you can find your favorite diner or new café on the block.

Once a member, you can upgrade to include thousands more customer reviews in three categories: Nightlife, Hotels or Attractions. Search for that new hot spot, check out their Top Lists, read ZagatNews and get ZagatWire and Zagat To Go from your e-mail or mobile devices and you'll know where to go, and where to dine al fresco!

Hungry & Thirsty

CHAIN OF FOODS

Top Secret Recipes
make all chain food favorites at home
www.topsecretrecipes.com

This one defines WAY COOL. Part info, part kitch, part anarchy! Top Secret Recipes describes itself as "…creating kitchen clones of America's favorite brand namc foods." Inspired by a chain letter prank about Mrs. Field's Cookies, TSP became the place to find scores of original "clone" recipes, while sharing cooking secrets and food stories.

Check out The Sleuth File and find out about the world's greatest hamburger. Better yet, head straight to recipes and type in a brand. You just may find that Colonel-fella's secret recipe. There are many free recipes but there are also recipes you can buy for only 79 cents. Ray Kroc would be proud.

ASIAN

DOESN'T HOISIN SAUCE SOUND LIKE A JERRY LEWIS WORD?

Asian Food Grocer
quality asian food, competitive prices
www.asianfoodgrocer.com

Living on both coasts (Peter-Los Angeles, Jim-New York) it is relatively easy to find specialty items when it comes to ethnic cuisines. Those living in Fon du Loc, Wisconsin may not find the same variety in their local stores. Enter Asian Food Grocer, an amazing resource of Asian products, edible or otherwise, serving both the food industry and folks like us for over 40 years.

Need Panko breadcrumbs? Order up a bag or get 6 at a big discount, because they sell wholesale and retail. They'll even ship frozen food by 2nd day air. Now, where's the hoisin sauce…hey, Dean!

BAKING

EVER WONDER ABOUT BREAD?

The Fresh Loaf
news and info for bakers and bread enthusiasts
www.thefreshloaf.com

We do. Sometimes, the perfect meal is a crispy baguette, a chunk of Stilton and rich, red Port (thanks,

Dad, for sharing that fondness). Take off those oven mitts and check out The Fresh Loaf. A community of bakers and artisan bread enthusiasts, a trip to their site and you'll find all you need to learn to bake or share the tips that you know.

There's a great Lessons section, along with Book Reviews, Recipes and Blogs. You'll have to be a member to post comments, recipes or a baker's blog, but it is free. Join, and you can actually post a picture of those smoked Cajun pork chops you made last night. Go on, show off!

CAFFEINE

ALL THINGS CAFFEINATED

Energy Fiend
get the lowdown on your favorite pick-me-up
www.energyfiend.com

Any site that has a Death by Caffeine calculator gets a place on this list. The folks at Energy Fiend bring you the numbers, knowledge and nonsense about anything that contains caffeine. They don't discriminate. Drinks, candy, sweets, if it's got caffeine, you can read about it. You can also compare which product will give you the biggest "buzz."

The death theme (tongue-in-cheek) takes the caffeine question even further with their Death by Penguin Mints category. Of course, the list of fully caffeinated candies and sweets is there for you to check, making sure you get the dose you need to get through the day.

CANDY

FEELIN' GROOVY

Groovy Candies
retro candy from the 50's through 80's
www.groovycandies.com

Time for a pop (rocks) quiz? Anyone remember Zagnut Bars? Atomic Fireballs? How about Boston Baked Beans? (And yes, they were candy.) You can find them AND order them all at Groovy Candies, the web home for nostalgic and retro candies. You'll get a sugar rush just visiting all your favorite childhood candies. They actually had individual packs of Chuckles!

We could list the endless assortment of sugary (and sugar-free) delights, but we'll leave that to you to browse the memories of the corner candy store. They have great gift ideas, too, from retro candy grab bags to candies for all occasions.

CHEESE

BRING ON THE FROMAGE

Fromages.com
the best of french cheeses
www.fromages.com

But fret not, mon ami, the fabulous French fromage you crave is a mere click (plus delivery) away from your table. Fromages.com invites you to discover these remarkable cheeses origins by learning their history and, of course, tasting them at home. There is a dedicated area for industry professionals to enter their cheese shop.

Search their vast selection of cheeses. Order them individually or purchase one of their cheese trays, with all the tasty decisions made for you, leaving you with the most important decision of all. Which wine do I open?

"LITHUANIAN BEAVER CHEESE?"

Murray's Cheese
over 60 years of great cheese
www.murrayscheese.com

"Not today, sir, no." They don't make cheese shops like the one in the famous Monty Python sketch. But they do make them like Murray's in NYC, the greatest cheese shop in the world! Perhaps a bit of hyperbole, but this Greenwich Village store has been an institution in New York since 1940!

The internet version is every bit its' equal, just not quite as odiferous. Proprietor Rob Kaufelt serves up over 250 cheeses. You can join the cheese of the month club, sign up for cheezE-mail, or find out when the next cheese appreciation course is being taught in NYC. If you can't get there, just get to your computer and order a slice of The Big Apple with Murray's Cheese. Now, shut that bloody bouzouki up!!!

CHOCOLATE

THE CHOCOHOLIC BUNNY SEZ...

Jacques Torres, Mr. Chocolate
champagne truffles and crème-filled dreams
www.mrchocolate.com

Jacques Torres is Mr. Chocolate. Don't believe us, Google his name. Or for that matter, try one of his reality-altering confections. He specializes in hand-crafted chocolates. They are exquisite, fresh, and free of artificial flavors and preservatives. Aside from these delectable morsels, his site offers a wonderful FAQ on chocolate, its cooking and storing.

Words are so inadequate if you have never tasted these decadent delights. He sells both wholesale and retail, and if you are ever in Manhattan or Brooklyn, you can go to one of his factories/stores and see, smell, then taste the magic when you enter. Warning: You may never want to leave…

COFFEE

BEAN THERE

The Coffee Review
world's leading coffee buying guide
www.coffeereview.com

Coffee expert, author and co-founder Kenneth Davids has created a one of a kind site dedicated to educate and entertain coffee drinkers. Not only that, but it's an invaluable tool to the coffee industry, offering them a chance to see how their product does based on objective, blind reviews from top industry leaders in the specialty coffee industry.

What does that mean to us the caffeine enthusiast? Check out the reviews of your favorite bean, blend or purveyor and see how they stack up to the competition. Better than that, you may fall upon a new favorite or an old friend. Either way, this is a WAY COOL site for coffee drinkers everywhere.

CREOLE/CAJUN

DOES YOUR BOUCHE NEED AMUSING?

Louisiana Lagniappe
your source for louisiana products
www.lalagniappe.com

By definition, "a "lagniappe" means an unexpected gift, a little something extra. Well, this family operated business in Hanhville, LA more than gives us our share of lagniappes on this site. They offer top quality Louisiana, Creole and Cajun products and stand behind all they sell with a money back guarantee. Along with food items, you can purchase cookers, fryers, even L.S.U. merchandise. Go Tigers!

Browsing through the edible selections, we found praline sweets, pecan brittle as well as an assortment of spices, dry rubs and mixes to make your Louisiana cookin' both tasty and authentic. Anytime is a good time for a Louisiana Lagniappe!

HEY JOE, WHATCHA GONNA DO WITH THAT GUMBO IN YOUR HAND?

The Creole and Cajun Recipe Page
let the good times roll!!!
www.gumbopages.com/recipe-page.html

This impressive Louisiana, Creole and Cajun food portal extraordinaire is a subset of The Gumbo Pages, a site dedicated to the preservation of New Orleans culture. Site creator Chuck Taggart, a native New Orleanian, has created pages upon pages that will make your mouth water just by reading them, and reading what is offered here is a must.

His passion for the tradition of Creole and Cajun cuisine is clearly evident in the detail in which he shares in his descriptions and recipes. Go to Basics and you'll see what we mean. Each step is detailed, to deliver the flavor, love and soul of the unique and resilient New Orleans, Louisianan.

DESSERT

EXTREME ICING

Mike's Amazing Cakes
cake making to the max
www.mikesamazingcakes.com

Executive Chef Mike McCarey has been making customized, highly creative cakes for all occasions for 23 years. The website has few pages but is chock full of great photos of his past creations. Each one comes with an explanation of why that cake was made.

Categories for his designer cakes are Wedding, Personal Occasion or Special Event. MAC is located in Redmond, WA and will deliver locally 7 days a week. They will also ship anywhere in the world but require at least two weeks' notice.

TANGERINE AND RACOON

E-Creamery

create custom-made ice cream, delivered!

www.ecreamery.com

Welcome to cold, creamy Nirvana! E-Creamery lets you build the perfect dessert and delivers it to your door. Imagine creating your very own ice cream flavor from scratch. You decide how much milk-fat, then add your favorite flavors. Not done? Add fruit, candy or a variety of toppings to your creation.

The best part (next to the eating) is you get to name your flavor! You can keep it to make re-ordering easy, or even have your named flavor sent to a friend. Even if you're feeling creatively uninspired, try one of EC's best selling combinations. They are sure to give you that ice cream freeze we all know and love, and taste much better than the flavor in our title.

KEY LIME PIE...ON A STICK!

Blond Giraffe
award-winning key lime pies
www.blondgiraffe.com/piepop.htm

No, really! Key lime pie on a stick! We can only imagine how great it tastes, and not sure why we haven't ordered them yet. Blond Giraffe makes award-winning (and you can see them on the site) key lime pie out of its main location in Key West, Florida.

You can also purchase key lime rum cake and Maté, a Brazilian coffee alternative. Create an on-line account (free) and start ordering a little slice (literally) of sweet and tart heaven.

PIE! HOW ARE YOU?

The Pie Gourmet
flaky delights from virginia
www.piegourmet.com

Here's another gem of a local bakery that ships nationally that we wanted to spotlight. *The Washington Post* called The Pie Gourmet from West Vienna, Virginia "a gem among local bakeries." Judging by their menu, whatever pie you may love, they probably make. They offer a selection of over 50 types of fruit or cream pies. There are also 8 different sugar-free pies from which to choose

If savory is more the order of the day, TPG offers a dozen or more dinner pies and quiches, like classics Chicken Pot Pie or Crab and Mushroom Quiche.

Toss in some of their lunch, dinner or dessert specialty items, order up and your dessert needs will be gratefully satisfied.

GREEK

IT'S ALL GREEK TO US

Greek Cuisine
break greek bread, not plates
www.greekcuisine.com

When we were kids, Mom always said, "learn about your heritage when you get older." And if you're Greek, to learn is to taste. Greek Cuisine.com is a subset of GreekShops.com, delivering quality and hard to find Greek products around the world. GC offers four choices to help you appreciate the food of our family's heritage: Cooking, Restaurants And Dining, Cookbooks, and Food/Delicacies.

Their restaurant portal is a terrific collection of Greek restaurants from around the world. Try (if you're not too busy) making Avgolemono soup from the Recipes link. Grandma Betty put chicken in her Avgolemono, and boy, did it taste good. In fact, if you peek ahead to page 79, we've shared her recipe with you.

HEALTHY FOODS

H IS FOR HEALTHY

World's Healthiest Foods
eat and cook healthy, feel great
www.whfoods.com

The George Mateljan Foundation for the World's Healthiest Foods is a not-for-profit organization dedicated to discover and share information without the influence of commercial interests. The aim is to insure we get scientific, unbiased information on nutrition and how we can manage to eat better in today's fast food world.

A wide range of topics is covered in three main categories to learn about and put to use in your everyday life. Check out their In-Home Cooking Demo, a step-by-step slide show for prep and cooking or find out what "organically grown" really means. Either way, eat healthy, live longer and give them a click.

GARDEN OF EATING

Slow Food Movement
local, traditional, diverse
www.slowfood.com

This Slow Food movement was pioneered by Carlo Patrini in Italy. A response to the insane world of bland, institutionalized fast food, the Slow Food Movement mission is to defend biodiversity in the food supply while re-educating the populous to the joys of eating, the importance of caring where their food comes from and support of those local farmers and their products. The organization proudly has over 80,000 members worldwide and growing, literally.

The site is teeming with information and education on this self-proclaimed "eco-gastronomy faction". There are opportunities to partake in events and conferences, articles from the movement around the globe and a section on the Slow Food Foundation of Biodiversity, which funds projects supporting regional gastronomic heritage. Take some time to read, to taste, perchance to dream....of food as it relates to your community.

INGREDIENTS

ALL THINGS GRATED AND SMALL

Adriana's Caravan
every ingredient for every recipe
www.adrianascaravan.com

Adriana's Caravan is the type of store you'd want to have in your neighborhood. Whatever you need, whenever you need it, there it is. No need petitioning the town fathers to open one up, just click on AC and have your shopping list ready. They will ship you products from all over the world, and the variety is endless. Spices, herbs, grains, chiles, oils, we can go on and on.

Proprietor Rochelle Zabarkes also offers many sumptuous gift baskets to mark that special occasion. Also available for purchase are cookbooks, tableware and, our favorite, truffle products. So, go around the culinary world from your office chair, because there is no need to walk a mile to Adriana's Caravan.

ITALIAN

RIGATONI SOPRANO

I Love Pasta
national pasta association
www.ilovepasta.org

From Alfredo to Ziti, everybody loves pasta (and Raymond). The National Pasta Association wants to make sure you're getting your share of nutritional facts as well as recipes on this site. They'll help you learn new ways to spice up some tried and true Italian recipes.

Photos accompany many of the recipes, with simple and easy methods. At the bottom there is a nutritional breakdown per serving provided. They even have a Pasta Improv Chart for you to mix and match what's in the fridge into a hearty and healthy meal.

LOS ANGELES

PUSHING THE BORDERS OF GREAT TASTE

The Two Hot Tamales
border grill and ciudad restaurants
www.marysueandsusan.com

If you don't know the Two Hot Tamales, then you are Doug and Tony from the Time Tunnel. Mary Sue Milliken and Susan Feniger have wowed mouths with their bold flavors and strong culinary statements for over 25 years. You may know them from TV or their cookbooks. Southern Californians have known them for decades.

City Restaurant changed the face and plates of Los Angeles dining. Currently, Border Grill in Santa Monica features the rich and savory tastes of Mexico. This cantina reset the bar for all other gourmet Mexican restaurants to follow. Downtown at Ciudad, patrons clamor for their authentic South American fare. Their site is cool, but the Border Girls are WAY COOL.

THE VIBRATION OF THE VIOLET FLAME

Inn of the Seventh Ray
organic delights, esoteric wisdom, cool gazebo
www.innoftheseventhray.com

Steeped in local history, the Inn of the Seventh Ray Restaurant serves organically grown foods and grains primarily from local farms. Soups are the Inn's own recipes and made with fresh herbs. Wines are offered from small, local wineries known for their care. There are alcohol-removed wines also available.

The Inn serves brunch and dinner, while also offering wedding packages and party planning. Aprés meal, browse The Spiral Staircase, a new age store with unique gifts. Enter The Inn and you'll be California dreamin' in no time.

MUSHROOMS

A MUSHROOM WITH A VIEW

Marché Aux Delices
get fresh, wild mushrooms overnight
www.auxdelices.com

Will Rogers said, "I never met a mushroom I didn't like!" He didn't really say that, but you will, when you taste the amazing earthy delights Amy and Thierry Farges bring to you. Marché Aux Delices is a family-owned company where you can order some of the world's finest, wild mushrooms. The Family Farges fungi fun does not stop there, authoring the Mushroom Lover's Mushroom Cookbook and Primer.

The gourmet treats continue, as truffles and truffle oil are also available, or try their porcini oil drizzled over....anything! Can't decide what to get? Try a seasonal mushroom sampler. Mad about mushrooms? You will be, when you march over to the Marché Aux Delices website.

NEW YORK

I'LL MAKE HIM AN ARTHUR HE CAN'T REFUSE

Arthur Avenue Specialties
on-line italian specialties source
www.arthuravespecialties.com

Everybody knows Little Italy, but New Yorkers know about Arthur Avenue in the Bronx, where you can get some of the best Italian food this side of Mama's kitchen. Arthur Avenue Specialties delivers great Italian food and products from no single warehouse, insuring quality as well as variety and freshness every time you order.

Choose from an array of Italian cured meats, cheese and bread, dried pasta, fresh meats and various and sundry grocery items. Olives and tomatoes are also available. Open up some vino and order up your AA specialties!

THE GREAT WHITEFISH WAY

Zabar's
blintzes over broadway for 70 years
www.zabars.com

What bag would you wear on your arm to show the world you have great taste? New Yorkers know it's a Zabar's bag, because it's most likely filled with gourmet treats, caviar, cheeses or better yet...smoked fish on a bagel! What started as an appetizer counter turned into Zabar's, the NYC gourmet emporium at 80th and Broadway for over 70 years.

From their own roasted coffee to the deli counter, to the housewares section, wander and shop around their site just as you would on a Sunday morning in The Big Apple. No recipes for rugelach here, just the opportunity to buy pounds of it and all the other delectable foods that has made Zabar's what it is today, a tasty slice of NYC food history.

SODA/POP

LET THE CARBONATION NATION RISE

Bev Net
beverage-oriented media company
www.bevnet.com

This site comes at you like a case of Jolt Soda, but we couldn't leave out anything that is dedicated to America's number one beverage, soda, or soda pop, or just pop or Coke (as they say in Atlanta). BevNet reviews non-alcoholic, ready-to-drink beverages, providing breaking news to and about the beverage industry.

Over 2,000 reviews have been posted since the company began in 1996. BevBlog and BevBoard are where discussions can range from industry trends to complaints and rants about the current state of carbonated affairs. So pop open a pop and see what you're drinking, thanks to BevNet.

SPICES

CUMIN SIDE AND PLAY!

The Epicentre
spice marketplace
www.theepicentre.com

This spice portal is filled with information on well known and hard-to-find exotic spices. This site is a little ad-heavy but it's loaded with answers, options and products to make your life tastier. Their depth of information is worth the read, especially if you are new to some cooking techniques. Their Conversion table is perfect for the math-impaired.

The Encyclopedia Of Spices is a page that needs to be bookmarked for easy reference. The Spice Trade offers interesting articles on said subject and the Wine Page may teach you to know what type of wine pairs well with the mastic you just used in your dessert.

KALUSTYAN AND DELIVER

Kalustyan's
landmark for fine specialty foods
www.kalustyans.com

Though we may have a playful, NYC-bias, but one walk into Kalustyan's and it's like you're in the United Nations of Food and Spices. Since 1944, they have brought some of the world's greatest flavors to the world's greatest chefs and home cooks alike.

The mainstay of Kalustyan's spices come from the Middle East and India, but the rest of the world is well represented in many categories of items for purchase. Coconut Products, Chutneys And Condiments, Gourmet and Sub-Continental Foods give you an idea of their variety. Spice up your life and meals with the real deal, Kalustyan's.

TURKEY

THE OTHER, OTHER WHITE MEAT

Eat Turkey
the perfect protein
www.eatturkey.com

The National Turkey Federation (no, really) is the national advocate for all things turkey (trimmings, optional), as well as a member organization making sure we all get the best bird for Thanksgiving AND all year long. We are big turkey fans (actually, we're big everything). This site is loaded with plenty of great stuff for the consumer, while allowing you to take a peek at the industry from its' own point of view.

But recipes are why foodies like to surf and Eat Turkey will give you lots of low fat, delicious options for turkey lovers. Tired of just roasting? Click on "deep fry turkey" to get started! (This may be the year ol' Tom gets fried.) Bored with the same chicken soup? Gobble up some Turkey Tortilla Soup!

VINO

SIMPLY IRRESISTABLE

Andrea Robinson
first lady of the vine
www.andreaimmer.com

Andrea Robinson (formerly Andrea Immer) is one of only 14 female Master Sommeliers in the world.

Her first book, *Great Wines Made Simple*, established her as one of America's top wine authors. Her real-world approach to wine appreciation blended with her natural effervescence and extraordinary knowledge makes her site a must destination for all wine lovers.

The site both works as a reference book and a workbook. Membership allows you a much broader range of WAY COOL tools. Her Food and Wine Pairing Tool lets you enter your dish into the database, and up pops the cork on the perfect wine to accompany it. Choose the wine first, and see what meal tastes even better when paired with Andrea's selection.

"GIVE ME WINE, WINE, I NEED MY INTRA-VINO"

Astor Wines and Spirits
wines, spirits, events and tastings
www.astoruncorked.com

A Greenwich Village landmark since 1946, Astor Wines and Spirits for decades has brought the largest selections of wine to New Yorkers. They now bring their vast knowledge and great prices to all those with internet access. Try their Food And Wine Matchmaker, pairing your perfect meal with the perfectly wonderful wine from Astor's impressive collection.

You can shop by price range, grape variety, vintage, region, etc. Every Tuesday they pick a region and markdown all wines by 15%. Each month they highlight the Top Ten for Under $10. With bargains like that, the money you save on wines can let you take a trip to NYC and visit Astor!

"I NEED IT EVERY DAY-O"

Wine Spectator Online
learn more, drink better
www.winespectator.com

We agree with the Hall and Oates lyrics in our last two titles. If you do, then you probably have a subscription to *The Wine Spectator*. You still need to check out their incredible site. Categories include Editor's Picks, Learn Wine and Travel & Dining. TWS offers a monthly or yearly membership to enhance your on-line experience with them.

We believe their membership is worth it for they have over 164,000 wine ratings to go along with membership and web exclusive columns, travel recommendations and food/wine pairing tips. A subscription to *The Wine Spectator* has been a long standing Christmas gift in the Spellos family.

IN VINO WE REALLY VERITAS

Best Cellars
making wine fun
www.bestcellars.com

This site is fun. Period. Any wine site that has categories such as Fuzzy, Luscious or Juicy just plain gets it. Education and entertainment do not have to be mutually exclusive and Best Cellars gets this concept. Their Oneo File will answer many of your questions. Read about grape varieties like the Black Muscat or Fumé Blanc.

Not sure what you like? Get in touch with your inner wine self and take their quiz. They'll even give you a few recipes to match with some drink ideas. Best Cellars has seven stores where they offer wine tastings, weekly events and special offers.

LAWRENCE WELK, ANYONE?

Champagne Magic
for champagne lovers everywhere
www.champagnemagic.com

Champagne Magic is like going to Sparkling Wines 101. It is maintained by someone whose love for the carbonated grape extends far beyond the bottle or the taste. There is so much to learn and love just by going through all the pages. Find out about history, varietals, even book a trip to Champagne, France.

The tone of the site is one of a champagne lover who speaks from the heart. "In general Champagne does not keep for decades, and is worth nothing at all to a collector unless it has been stored in perfect cellar conditions since purchase. So if you have an old bottle stored for fifteen years on the mantelpiece, open it with your fingers crossed as soon as possible and drink it." We most assuredly agree. Cheers!

DON'T BE A FREDO OF ITALIAN WINE

Rubicon Estate
francis ford coppola's winery
www.rubiconestate.com

The Rubicon Estate website is as epic and all encompassing, as a Francis Ford Coppola film. Formerly Niebaum-Coppola on the historic Inglenook property, Rubicon Estate was renamed after its' flagship wine (which we adore) to celebrate the reuniting by Coppola of all the original vineyards plus restoring winemaking to the Chateau (take the tour).

We have had the pleasure of visiting the winery a few times. We've packed a great lunch from Dean & DeLuca's in Napa, bought a bottle of Rubicon at the Chateau and sat and just enjoyed the moment. Then we wandered through the museum, had more of Francis' vino and walked some more. Why aren't we telling you about the site? Why aren't you there now? Avanti!!!

Educational & Reference

OFF TO SEE THE WIZARD

Alton Brown (a.k.a. The Waffler…oops)
food science champion, teacher, entertainer
www.altonbrown.com

If Alton Brown was actually one of his food science projects, your ingredients list might look like this: Take one part Mr. Wizard, one part techno-geek, one part Jonathan Winters and two parts Southern gentleman, Shake with a multi-tasker and serve to millions of satisfied fans in books, on television and around the world. You know him from his long (7 seasons) running Good Eats on The Food Network, the half-hour food encyclopedia of fun, facts and fawning over food. He has won the James Beard Award twice for Best Cookbook (reference) and was 2004 Cooking Teacher of the Year, as voted by the *Bon Appétit* American Food Awards.

His website is as entertaining and informative as the man himself. There is a page just dedicated to his motorcycle ensemble and gear that he used while shooting Feasting on Asphalt, his 2006 summer "on the road" show. You can purchase the "death to uni-taskers" t-shirt (we love that one), get your very own salt cellar, or go to the Knowledge page and follow the links to your heart's content.

We've dedicated a whole page to Alton, because he really has inspired us to explore the science behind the art of our own cooking. Questioning why can teach us how, and from there we have the freedom and the confidence to create anew. It is important to surround yourself with people of passion and purpose in life. Well, Alton Brown certainly tops that menu. Thanks, AB, we'd be glad to call you friend…or even for dinner! (and sorry about The Waffler thing…)

CAREER

DO THEY RING THE SCHOOL BELL PEPPERS?

Cooking Schools Online
culinary school information and links
www.cooking-schools.net

How does one choose a culinary institute? Cooking Schools Online lets you easily click and find the numerous cooking schools and culinary arts programs around the country. This site is simple and direct. Not many whistles and bells, nothing flashes at you, but you are given a quantity of opportunities to go out and learn your craft and skills

There's also a Cooking Resource Guide, where you can take at peek at some of the many and sundry food sites that seem to grow geometrically on the web. There are many links to food and recipe sites, as well as those with a food industry bias.

I'M VINE, HOW'S BY YOU?

Wine and Hospitality Jobs
get a job now in wine country
www.winecountryjobs.com

Tired of the rat race? Ready to give up that asphalt jungle for the lushness of the vineyard? Then the folks at Wine and Hospitality Jobs have answered your call of the wild (well, maybe the valley)! The site basically is set up for job seekers and employers to make a love, er, food connection! Employers can post jobs, search for recruits or work with their consulting team to tailor any plan they need.

As for the job seekers, you can post your resume or receive the free newsletter about great career opportunities at some of the nation's finest vineyards and restaurants, including The French Laundry, perhaps the Spellos Brothers' all-time favorite.

LAISSEZ LES BON TEMPS ROULEZ!!!

The New Orleans School of Cooking
classes, country store and joe's stuff
www.neworleansschoolofcooking.com

The first thing we love about this site, is you can click on "Great Cajun Tunes" and music of the Bayou will accompany you as you shop. NOSC has introduced folks from all over the world to the joys and spices of Louisiana cooking. Their Creole/Cajun cooking team will teach you to prepare gumbo, jambalaya, and other mouth watering dishes.

We also love this site because we've been cookin' with their dry rub seasoning called Joe's Stuff for many years. Rub up your pork chops and make them, as Emeril would say, "happy, happy, happy." They also sell Joe's Hot Stuff, marinades, mixes and all you could need for a Bayou Blast!

GETTING DOWN TO BUSINESS

Chef 2 Chef
culinary portal
www.chef2chef.net

This is no cloying fan site, or a homage to a favorite inspiration, but a no-nonsense food industry portal, chock full of great information for the food service industry. Anything a chef or restaurateur could possibly need they can find thanks to Chef 2 Chef. The home page alone has food service news feeds, job postings, culinary student forums and more.

C2C also has a unique Chef Of The Month page, where you can sample the recipes from 70 famous chefs, chef celebrities, TV chefs and rising star chefs. This industry-driven site is a must for all serious foodies

COOKBOOKS

HOME, HOME IN THE RANGE

101 Cookbooks
exploring cookbooks, one recipe at a time
www.101cookbooks.com

As far as we're concerned, you own 101 cookbooks, you know something about food. Author/photographer Heidi Swanson has taken her passion for cooking and created a great site that is elegant and smartly written. She chronicles her journey through life's kitchens, learning new techniques and ingredients, inspiring cooks to do the same.

Of course, there are links to the 101 cookbooks on Amazon.com, where you can own the one you love. Heidi's site also includes forums, cooks' journals, loads of great recipes and an opportunity to take classes in the Bay Area with her. This tasty site needs to be in your bookmarks!

PUT THE BISCUIT IN THE BASKET

Jessica's Biscuit®
the cooks, cooking and food site
www.ecookbooks.com

Obscure Keith Olbermann reference notwithstanding, Jessica's Biscuit® is neither about hockey pucks or biscuits. JB has the word's largest cookbook inventory - over 13,000 titles. These are not just your book store chain titles, either. There are many hard to find and out of print books that may make or break that special meal you're planning.

JB offers all these cookbooks at huge discounts every day. You can also shop for other products like DVD's and posters, or check out recipes at the chef's corner, with links and bios to some of your favorite food authors and chefs. For those who like a hard copy (pliable, really) of all this info, JB will gladly send you their cornucopian catalog of cookbooks.

EDUCATIONAL

KNOWLEDGE IS GOOD

The Culinary Institute of America
66 years of excellence
www.ciachef.edu

So spoke Emil Faber. And you will love the knowledge you gain if you are lucky enough to train at The Culinary Institute of America, the world's premiere culinary college. They offer various degree programs, most notably their CIA bachelors or associates degree in Culinary Arts or Baking and Pastry Arts! CIA West offers many of the same degree programs as the Hyde Park, NY campus, plus a wine studies program.

We have been up to CIA's Napa Valley campus. Talk about the hallowed kitchen halls of learning and eating! Don't miss indulging at Wine Spectator's Greystone Restaurant, where you can walk by the herb gardens that will be used to season your meal!

I MYTH THE OLD DAYS...

Kitchen Myths
debunking culinary urban legends
www.pgacon.com/KitchenMyths.htm

We include this site in our collection because the author's goal is to separate cooking facts from fiction. He documents all findings with either links or book sources. For instance, does cold water boil faster than warm water? Are you sure you know the correct answer?

Aside from culinary myth busting, KM also poses and examines some other kitchen questions, like: Water over milk when making scrambled eggs or omelets? How do thickening agents differ? Can you make a really good cup of tea in the microwave? Hey, we got one. Does gorgonzola reek if no one's there to smell it?

"WHAT'S ANOTHER WORD FOR THESAURUS?"

The Cook's Thesaurus
visual references to foods you may or may not know
www.foodsubs.com

Comedian Steven Wright's quote is still funny, but, there's nothing funny about The Cook's Thesaurus, an on-line food encyclopedia, covering thousands of ingredients and kitchen tools. With pictures and descriptions of each entry, the CT also offers up pronunciations, synonyms and suggested substitutions.

They highlight an Ingredient of the Month to go along with their food database. It's another no-frills site, offering up helpful hints in lieu of opinions and conjectures. Don't know what kind of cookie a Corico is? You will soon.

AND THE WINNER IS.....

The James Beard Foundation
celebrating the appreciation of culinary excellence
www.jamesbeard.org

For 20 years now, the James Beard Foundation's mission is to celebrate and nurture America's culinary heritage and diversity. From their delicious dinners and workshops held at The Beard House to the 16th annual JBF Awards, this site shows all the amazing accomplishments by this foundation.

In 2005, JBF awarded over $250,000 to 86 scholarship recipients. They support Spoons Across America, providing nutritional education to families and community-based programs. This prestigious, not-for-profit organization remains the gold standard in the honoring and supporting of the ever growing appreciation for the culinary arts.

ARE DOUG AND TONY STILL IN THE TIME TUNNEL?

The Food Timeline
food history and reference research service
www.foodtimeline.org

Imagine going back in time to find out how Thomas Jefferson made his ice cream? The Food Timeline makes this, and so much more, possible. TFT is an independent research project by a reference librarian out to help students and teachers with food history questions and facts.

The timeline is great to explore, allowing you to click on foods and find their land of origin. Did you know that when Pop Tarts first came on the market in 1964 they were sold in the Baked Goods aisle? (we better get a nutritionist…)

THEY REALLY DO A BODY GOOD

Food Allergy & Anaphylaxis Network
raising public awareness to food allergies
www.foodallergy.org

Amidst all the fun we are having with these sites, it is important not to neglect the ones that truly help people (more on that later in the book). FAAN, established in 1991, has a membership of over 30,000, both medical and everyday people, dedicated to aid and educate all those with food allergies and anaphylaxis. They have worked directly with government agencies and policy makers on many local and national initiatives.

A fourteen member Advisory Board, compromised of medical leaders in the aforementioned field, oversee all of FAAN publications for scientific accuracy. There is a membership fee for their newsletters and publications, but all the important information is free and easy to find.

FOOD SCIENCE

EXPLORATORIUM - PA PUM PUM

The Accidental Scientist
the science of cooking
www.exploratorium.edu/cooking

A vast, totally hands-on exploration of science and the senses, The Accidental Scientist, the web version of San Francisco's Museum of Science, Exploratorium, makes learning both entertaining and informative. You can Ask The Inquisitive Cooks a question, sniff around in their Seasonings page (take the tour of the spice map) or choose some new reading in Books To Devour.

One of the best features is their archived Webcasts, showing the Iron Science Teacher leading demonstrations in the Exploratorium kitchens. Check out the site, then call your travel agent and visit the museum. And bring the kiddies….

SOME LIKE IT HOT

The Chile Pepper Institute
new mexico state university
www.chilepepperinstitute.org

Others like it *really* hot. Then there's Wilbur Scoville, but that's a whole other story. The keepers of the flame are housed at New Mexico State University, College of Agriculture and Home Economics. Since 1992, the not-for-profit Chile Pepper Institute has been a recognized research organization, dedicated to educating the world about chiles.

TCI needs public support in many ways: by sending articles, links or clippings, by donating money or even time. Become a long-standing member or donor and you may be honored with a chile-decorated ceramic tile in the Institute's Hall of Flame. You can also heat up your life with many items in the Chile Shop. So, how hot do you like it?

KITCHEN SUPPLIES

WHERE THE BLUE PLATE SPECIAL REALLY IS BLUE PLATES

The Chef's Catalog
for the home chef or the culinary professional
www.chefscatalog.com

This on-line version of the famous CHEFS Catalog is a great way to stock up on all your kitchen supply needs. Almost all the major brands are represented, from All-Clad to Wusthof, with a picture of each product. They give you gift ideas categorized by price, occasion, and even recipient.

CHEFS also provides recipes from their catalog. You'll get stuffed just dreaming up recipe variations you'll be able to create with the new kitchen hardware or software you can purchase. Don't forget to create a registry while you're surfing their site, the holidays are coming soon, and that special someone just may need to know what to get you!

I'M WILLIAMS, HE'S SONOMA

Williams-Sonoma
the place for cooks
www.williams-sonoma.com

In 1956, when Chuck Williams opened his first store in Sonoma, CA, he sold only French cookware. Fifty years later W-S is the premiere specialty retailer of home furnishings in the U.S. This site lets you lose yourself in fantasies of cooking in your own "kitchen stadium," surrounded by all state-of-the-art gizmos and gadgets.

WAY COOL toys aside for now, the W-S site is filled with other goodies to buy for the kitchen and dining rooms. Great tips and ideas for entertaining abound (ooh, pumpkin bread with dates) and you can also use their registry. Hmm. Maybe we should leave OUR wish list here for you…

MAGAZINES

EPICURIOSITY WON'T KILL THE CAT

Epicurious
for people who love to eat
www.epicurious.com

Combining the resources of both *Gourmet* and *Bon Appétit*, this site is elegant and extensive, a wonderful companion for both magazines. It certainly stands on its own as one of the top gourmet recipe portals around.

Their illustrated, on-line guides will help you choose caviar or tell the right time to pick thyme. You can catch video clips of one of our faves, Michael Lomonaco from the Travel Channel's Epicurious TV. There are timely articles, hints on wine and cheese pairings, we can go on and on. Better yet, go there yourself and indulge your inner chef.

RECIPES FOR SUCCESS

Saveur
savor a world of authentic cuisine
www.saveur.com

Saveur is a truly unique magazine and website, with emphasis on heritage and tradition, focusing on home cooking from around the globe. Culinary adventures with a travel slant! You get to visit the places where the food and recipes originate made by the people who enjoy it everyday.

There is a wonderful archive of culinary traditions, where you can pick a destination anywhere in the world, and they take you to archived articles from the magazine about your favorite region or cuisine. We just finished reading an article about the Ouzo bars of Greece. What a surprise! What isn't a surprise is the top notch writing and recipes you find with *Saveur*.

IF FOOD BE THE MUSIC OF LOVE....

Food & Wine
companion site to their magazine
www.foodandwine.com

If you like the magazine (and we do), you'll love the site. Under the American Express umbrella, F&W has informative articles, mixed with Web Only recipes, and of course, offers you wonderful food-themed travel options. You can sample their restaurant guide when you don't feel like making one of the tempting recipes from their database.

The site does continually remind you to order two risk-free issues of the magazine, but when there are recipes like Pork Dumplings with Aged Black Vinegar, that seems like more than a fair trade. You can't go wrong with F&W!

PORTALS

MRS. PLUM IN THE KITCHEN WITH THE KNIFE

The Gourmet Sleuth
gourmet food and cooking resource
www.gourmetsleuth.com

The Gourmet Sleuth serves a variety of purposes. It is a highly focused directory, allowing the user to get to the info they need quicker. They help people indulge in their food passions, by writing articles on a variety of culinary topics, including recipes that take a very how-to approach.

TGS maintains a catalog of specialty or hard-to-get items that are not readily available elsewhere. Some of these items range from pot de crème cups to tortilla presses. They even have some fun categories like A Guy's Gotta Eat and Dog Treat Recipes (don't mix those up). So, go snooping over at The Gourmet Sleuth.

DID GRANNY SMITH LIKE APPLES?

Food Reference Website
food trivia, history, recipes and more
www.foodreference.com

This is the smorgasbord of food portals. No matter how much you partake, there will be a never-ending supply of choices from this site. Search for exotic drink recipes or recite the myriad of odes to food and poems. How about a listing of all food shows around the country? You can find that here.

There's a great list of gourmet food holidays, international cooking vacations, or info for that weekend at the vineyard. How about trying out some culinary-themed crossword puzzles? Need to find a review of that new cookbook that's on TV? You won't run out of things to search, because FRW has over 12,000 pages.

Goulash

EAT AT JOE'S

Road Food
memorable eateries along the high and back roads
www.roadfood.com

This is a WAY COOL site. Road Food.com is your gateway to great meals served by non-franchised eateries, a slice of local Americana to go with the big ol' slice of apple pie (heated and a la mode, of course). They feature over 1,000 diners, pancake houses, taco stands and the like, serving you a taste of local fare or your favorite comfort food.

There's Road Food News, plenty of reviews from small towns and big cities, a restaurants search engine, and photo of the restaurant (and meal) of the day. Become a Roadfood Insider (membership fee) and share info and favorites with over 40,000 other food lovers. If you're hungry for adventure both in life and at your meals, park it at Road Food.com

ASTRONAUT FOOD

FLY ME TO THE MOONPIE

Astronaut food
astronaut ice cream, space sticks
www.funkyfoodshop.com

If you have read this far, you're now in for some fun sites. We'll start with the folks at the Funky Food Shop. They sell astronaut ice cream, the freeze dried packets that have been a space-age dessert for over 4 decades. This will never replace our love of the real thing, but the FFS sells not only the standard issue tri-flavored bar, but now you can get freeze-dried ice cream sandwiches or mint chocolate chip.

For you high-flying non-dairy fans, FFS has freeze dried fruits: Astro Apples, Strawberries and Funky Peaches (perhaps a name change on that one). Want something different for dessert? Open up a bag of astronaut ice cream. It melts in your mouth, not in the zero-gravity vacuum of space!

BEER/ALE

DRINKERS OF THE WORLD...GET UP!

Campaign for Real Ale
advocating drinkers' rights since 1971
www.camra.org.uk

When you first check out this site, you say "drinkers rights?" But the Campaign for Real Ale (located in Great Britain) is really about saving the small pubs and breweries from the bland processed "beer" produced by the mega-breweries. They campaign for a "true pint," making sure drinkers are not shortchanged to the tune of £400 each year.

The little guy/big guy struggle is more than a parable at CAMRA. They are just as passionate about real ciders and perry (made from pears) and that the real versions are neither carbonated nor pasteurized. You can purchase the 34th edition of the Good Beer Guide, and find the great pubs of England from your own home.

BUDGET

GOT POWDERED MILK?

Hillbilly Housewife
low cost, home cooking from scratch
www.hillbillyhousewife.com

What can we say about Miss Maggie? Well, here's a quote from her website – "The recipes are tested in a real kitchen with hungry children. The ingredients are affordable and readily available in most areas."

Like many sites, her recipes come with her share of ideologies (but don't get us started). She'll show you how, with judicious shopping and reuse of another meal's ingredients (aka leftovers), you can feed a family of four on $70 per week! Let's say that again - $70 per week!!! If nothing else, this site should get you thinking dough. Spend less of it, make more of it (literally).

GOURMET HOLIDAYS

THE ROAD LESS EATEN

Active Gourmet Holidays
exceptional travel experiences
www.activegourmetholidays.com

Imagine learning to cook with Port…in Portugal! Active Gourmet Holidays offers you many wonderful Culinary and Wine Tour choices to Italy, France, Spain or Portugal combined with unique opportunities to learn to cook from some of the great chefs of their regions. AGH also has exquisite Outdoor Tours such as bike tours like The Cycling Gourmet in Tuscany.

If art is your passion, AGH brings you Art & Painting Tours, allowing the artist in you to be inspired where the masters created while enjoying the culinary masterpieces you'll experience on your European gourmet getaway.

MAMA MIA…NO, MAMA MARGARET!

Mama Margaret
italian cooking holidays
www.italycookingschools.com

Margaret is neither a mama, nor is she Italian, but don't let that stop you from visiting her site. "Mama" (as called by adoring clients) has been guiding people through cooking tours of Italy since 1995. She is a culinary veteran, having visited over 40 holiday cooking programs to assure only the finest for her tour members, meeting with chefs and accommodations, and of course, sampling the food.

You can take one of her preplanned cooking tours (Tuscany, Brunell and Vino Nobile Wine Country) or a specially tailored trip for food professionals and gourmet travelers alike. Some of Mama's favorite recipes are available on-line.

HARDWARE

FRY ME A RIVER

Quality Fryers
deep fryers and turkey fryers
www.qualityfryers.com

In our Turkey category in the Hungry and Thirsty chapter, we talk about always wanting to deep fry a turkey (we actually watched one being cooked in a play Off-Broadway). Quality Fryers specializes in the highest quality turkey fryers and accessories in the country. Their product line is not just limited to great aluminum or stainless steel cookware. They also bring you cast iron cookware, dutch ovens, single, double and triple burner cookers.

They have a very good assortment of cooking accessories, lids, baskets and all the hardware you will need to turn ol' Tom Turkey into, as Alton Brown might say, "something golden brown and delicious." Tell us how it comes out!

HOT SAUCE

BURN, BABY BURN

Insane Chicken
taste the insanity
www.insanechicken.com

With all the talk about global warming, the kind of heat we hope never goes away is hot sauce. The folks at Insane Chicken (the name alone gets them in our book) is an Internet retailer selling hot sauces, condiments, rubs and gifts, for folks who choose to live on the spicy side of the street. They feature a hot sauce of the month club, with a variety of mild to wild.

Aside from hot sauces, there are spicy marinades for jerk chicken, dry rubs for your favorite ribs, or try the 357 Mad Dog, the hottest sauce ever made, putting out 600,000 sizzlin' Scoville Units. If your eyes haven't already seared shut, click on the chick, the Insane Chicken will heat up your life!

HUMOR

"HOW Y'ALL ARE?"

Justin Wilson
bayou legend, humorist
www.justinwilson.com

That distinctive voice of Justin Wilson echoes his trademark greeting, welcoming you to his site. The world famous cookbook author, storyteller and American culinary legend passed on in 2001. His daughter Sara, who worked beside her father for 40 years, continues to make sure the world remembers Justin through purchase of many products.

Hear this Creole raconteur through comedy CD's and DVD's. Offered are his cookbooks, to go along with a line of sauces and his Wicked Cajun Pickles. He'll make your face smile and your belly happy, "we garontee!"

ICE CREAM

SYMPATHY FOR THE DEVILS FOOD CAKE

Ben and Jerry's
graveyard of forgotten flavors
www.benandjerrys.com/graveyard

Root Beer Float My Boat sank. Bovinity Divinity was not heavenly and Honey, I'm Home kept them on the couch. For every creamy B&J's flavor we've devoured, countless others either never caught on, or had their moment in the sun then melted. So, B&J dug up the Flavor Graveyard, the dearly departed dessert destination for former flavors.

A moment of silence for From Russian With Buzz. Say a kind word for Honey Apple Raisin Chocolate Cookie (honey flavor just not working). Can I get an amen from the cone-gregation for Peppermint Schtick? Now, go and pay your respects to this fun site. What S'mores could you need?

ON THE ROAD

EATING ON THE FLY

Airline Meals
all about airline food
www.airlinemeals.net

Those who travel primarily by "coach" domestically are saying, "What airline food?" but there is still a great deal of food, tasty and otherwise, being served by airlines all over the world. How do we know this? There are thousands of pictures of in-flight meals. This site has contributors from all over the world, putting a kitchen mirror up to the food the airlines are dishing out.

Check out Crew Meals (do they eat better than we do?), or Meals in Movies. (What was Anthony Hopkins eating on the plane in Hannibal?) Whatever you choose, stop over at this site but leave your bottled water at the gate.

RECIPES (VISUAL)

TOMMY, CAN YOU PEEL ME?

Visual Recipes
recipes with step-by-step pictures
www.visualrecipes.com

Ooh, pictures! We all remember as kids, if it doesn't look good, we won't eat it, or in this case, serve it. Each recipe on this site has multiple photos to take you through each step of the recipe. Layout is simple, though the site has many ads with the occasional pop-up (now popovers would be a tastier option).

A group of 50 or so users were on their Cooking Chat Forums one night we visited. There's also a cooking school portal categorized by state, and "what to look for" guidelines when choosing a culinary school. Now, where is that apple popover recipe?

SALAD DRESSING

WHO MADE THE SALAD DRESSING?

Salad Dressing Recipes
nothing but salad dressing recipes
www.nikibone.com/recipe/salad_dressings.html

This page, part of a personal website, echoes that often, function over form can truly prevail. This no-frills page has nothing but salad dressing recipes. Sixty-three to be exact. All simple and easy to make. Who needs those folks up at that hidden ranch, when Niki will help you make Creamy Herb, Cumin-Lime, or Classic Raspberry Vinaigrette?

If you click her recipe index, it will then take you to her recipe page, where she has an impressive 40 categories of recipes for all occasions. It's great to see another food fan share their passion. Stop by your green grocer and whip up a batch of dressing to go with your next meal.

SPAM

"SPAM, SPAM, SPAM, SPAM...."

SPAM
the one and only
www.spam.com

With the Python's hypnotic chant echoing in our heads, we bring to you the planet's most canned meat since 1937. Any baby boomer worth his sodium knows Spam from the canned food heydays of the 60's. Over 6 billion cans of Spam have been sold, and the Spammobile travels to over 675 events per year. That's a whole lotta luncheon meat!

Fret not, you health-nut naysayers out there, the Hormel Corp. has not forsaken you. There's Spam Less Sodium with 25% less sodium than the original, or try Spam Lite – 33% fewer calories and 50% less fat. More Spam you cry? Try Oven-Roasted Turkey or Smoked Flavor Spam. Join the Spam Fan Club and show the world you're spam-tastic!

TECHNOLOGY

WHAT'S THE FREQUENCY, KENNETH?

Vindigo City Guide
location-specific content to mobile devices
www.vindigo.com

In case Scotty and the crew of the Enterprise are out of range, Vindigo is your best bet for finding what you need, when you need it right in the palm of your hand. Vindigo City Guide brings you the who, what and where of restaurants, movies, museums and stores in major cities across America.

Can't find that restaurant that just got a great review? Vindigo gets you there, with full color maps, walking directions and local transit information. Select your restaurants by street, intersection or neighborhood or by features or cuisine types. Go to your meals, or get meals to go, courtesy of the Vindigo City Guide.

TOAST

A TOAST TO TOASTERS

The Toaster Museum Foundation
unusual internet museum
www.toaster.org

Ah, shades of the classic "House of Toast" sketch by Bob & Ray! (Look them up, you'll laugh!)

The story about how this museum came about is worth the read, as is the entire site. Part homage to American ingenuity and functional art, TMF hope to entertain as much as to educate, and we believe they do.

Take a tour of the Cyber Toaster Museum or check out the Interactive page, but don't load any slices into the CD-ROM drive. There are some truly unique pictures in the Toast(er) Art Gallery. They are a not-for-profit organization, so donations are welcome, whether monetary or electrical.

TV DINNERS

DINING BY TUBE-LIGHT

Swanson's 50th Anniversary Celebration
tv dinners from the source
www.swansonmeals.com/50th

Swanson celebrated 50 years of frozen TV dinners with this hip and retro looking tribute to one of their staples. In 1953, they introduced a hungry country to the TV Dinner. By the next year over 25 million were sold, like turkey on corn bread dressing, peas, mashed potatoes, done in minutes and served fast and hot.

They continued to branch out in 1969 to include their Frozen Breakfasts. Don't forget 1973, when Mean Joe Greene introduced Hungry Man Dinners. There are cool retro commercials you can watch, too. So go heat up a pot-pie and turn on the tube!

TWINKIES

THEY BLOW-ED UP REAL GOOD!

The T.W.I.N.K.I.E.S. Project
crème-filled science experiment
www.twinkiesproject.com

Well, you made it to the 99th Fabulous Food Website, so we figured we'd end it with a bang….literally! The T.W.I.N.K.I.E.S. project, Tests With Inorganic Noxious Kakes In Extreme Situations, lives up to its' acronym. Imagine - science experiments with Twinkies!!! Happy, happy, joy, joy. Fire, radiation, gravity – no test too tough for the Boys in Research over at Rice University.

Ponder the results when a 110 V standard AC current charges a Twinkie (is one singular, or is it collective?). Argue the results of the Radiation Test, or just spend a few minutes and realize, if your life is too dull, there are those living on the edge of reality who can take you places you never dared to dream….

Seven Course Finale

Admit it. We've all played a variation of this game. You're on a deserted island and you can only take three albums with you (vinyl, for you kids into "retro") or which three books would you bring or which three DEAL OR NO DEAL models….ah, you get the picture!

So, we thought about our favorite meals, then we narrowed it down to the perfect dinner party, then we finally decided upon the classic seven course meal to make our ultimate food indulgence meal. The seven courses, arguably speaking of course, are called: First Course, Soup Course, 1st Appetizer, 2nd Appetizer, Fish Course, Meat Course, Dessert. We picked the ultimate meal we have already eaten, but never in one sitting. But here - with no caloric constraints or even gastronomic orgy rituals of the ancient Romans to impede this fantasy menu, we present to you The Seven Course Finale - The Fabulous Spellos Brothers' take on the best meal ever!

The choices were so many, but with a singular criteria. We had both tasted and agreed on all the final picks, whether it be a family recipe (ours or our friends) or one we had in a restaurant. As in all "best of" lists, deciding what goes is half the fun. Don't agree with ours? Hey, the fun of this is to come up with your own, as well as now indulging in *our* Nine Wonders of the Modern Culinary World! Hey, smells like another book, but for now, just waft through these next few pages and enjoy what we've enjoyed tasting together over the years. We have published the recipes not previously published at the end of this chapter. Those we could not for legal reasons print, we have made sure you have a link, a phone number, or an address to contact to get the recipes.

We now present to you, The Seven Course Finale! Please raise your glasses so we can toast the.....what, you don't have any wine? Fret not, mon amis, we saved our secret favorite wine spot on the web until now!

The Napa Valley Winery Exchange (NVWE), www.nvwe.com, located in downtown San Francisco, is our very favorite wine store, both in person and on-line. The Leonardini family owns and runs this amazing place, which features wine gems for the area's smallest producers. These are rare and delicious California wines one cannot find at your local liquor store or mini-mart. Select by grape, region or vintage. We like the gift sets and wine samplers.

Now that the secret's out about NVWE and you have that spicy little number from Sonoma, (we're talkin' zinfandel, kids), let's belly up to the table and get ready for The Seven Course Finale! Read on and you better save room for dessert!!!

FIRST COURSE

Pearls and Oysters

The French Laundry, Yountville, CA

www.epicurious.com/recipes/recipe_views/105859

Tasting Thomas Keller's luscious first course at The French Laundry is akin to what eyes must feel when they gaze upon sheer beauty, or ears when they are caressed by the perfect harmony. Think we're waxing way too poetic about an appetizer? It's only just food, you snicker? Well, check when the Wine Train leaves for Yountville. We'll be up late waiting for your call…

SOUP COURSE

Grandma Betty's Avgolemono Soup

173rd St & Ft. Washington Ave., NYC, circa 1964

Our favorite cousin Niki Costidis helped Mom in recalling this recipe. Recollections of it differ from childhood, as the soup lends itself to certain varied interpretations. We've decided to go with the basic family recipe, which calls for orzo. Rice was very often used instead of orzo, and we're sure the recipe would differ greatly. Also, earliest recollections seem to also have chicken, sort of like a Greek chicken and rice with lemon and egg soup. We've even replaced the chicken with Chilean Sea Bass. Again, we've opted to share the most classic and traditional Spellos family Avgolemono.

1st APPETIZER

Crawfish and Andouille Sausage Gumbo

It's all about the roux, end of story. Jim's been know to grow a beard while stirring. Must have okra, another deal breaker in this recipe. The recipe is truly a mélange of favorite recipes, with our own spices and surprises. Layers of flavors and rice if you like.

We've made it for parties, we've made it for the hair and make-up departments on AMERICAN DREAMS. This gumbo is rich and tasty. Jim would like to add more vinegar to it, Peter would rather you just toss in more andouille!

2nd APPETIZER

Mom's Pastitsio

Taymil Road, New Rochelle, NY – childhood home 1966-1977

Our darling mother Diana, when asked about this Pastitsio she was preparing for dinner, once said to one of our friend's having supper with us, "Do you know what lasagna is? Well, it's nothing like that!" Gotta love her! Her version, probably with both Greek and Turkish influences from our grandparents, is the best, maybe because it was hers. We've even tinkered with variations, but this is the original recipe. Ah, that slightly crunchy béchamel topping over cinnamon laced chopped beef and tubular pasta, that mom placed neatly in a row. Wow. Wish we were kids again, if only for a minute....

FISH COURSE

Fresh Maine Lobster

Harraseeket Lunch and Lobster, Freeport, ME
At the Freeport Wharf - (207) 865-3535

This one is real simple. If you want Maine Lobster, you….very good, go to Maine! You'll never eat a better lobster than the one you saw them take out of the water 20 minutes ago. We mean the sea, not the fish tank in the front of Nicky's Clam House, Main St., U.S.A. Oh, yeah. Start off with the fried clams!

MEAT COURSE

Bayside Bunnie's Brisket O' Beef

Spellos/Messinger test kitchen, Bayside, NY

A brisket. A package of Lipton's Onion Soup mix. A bottle of Heinz' Chili Sauce. A can of Pepsi (no Coke). That's it. Stop laughing. We laughed. We made it. We wrestled over the final pieces. Serve with your favorite potato recipe and seasonal veggies, but you're not going to touch them. This melt-in-your-mouth caramelized wunderoast is beef lovers wonderland of flavors and texture. If you can make a better brisket of beef, we'll come right over and eat it. Promise. And hold the veggies.

DESSERT

Banana Cream Pie

Emeril's New Orleans Fish House, Las Vegas, NV
http://tinyurl.com/yxy68w

We'd never dream of telling a cardiologist how many times we've eaten this truly unbelievable dessert. Each time, it's been dessert heaven. We even made it one Christmas and it still was delicious. It is so darn good, it made our friend Mary Elizabeth McGlynn literally weep upon her first bite at Emeril's in Las Vegas. No, really. We cry tears of joy just thinking about that taste too, Mary Elizabeth!

NIGHTCAP

Prager 2003 Royal Escort Vintage Port

Prager Winery & Port Works, St. Helena, CA
www.pragerport.com

This has been our favorite place in Napa Valley for over a decade. Our father brought home port, both red and white, from a business trip to Portugal when were teenagers. It is a taste he loved and a tradition and passion we acquired, oddly enough.

Jim Prager and family, not only make the best line of ports and dessert wines this side of the galaxy, they are the nicest bunch of folks we've met along this journey. Jim Prager, Santa's stand-in, presides over the tastiest of tasting rooms, which, if you sneak behind the oak barrels, could hide you for days. They have two vineyard suites, B&B style. We've stayed. We've sipped. We've autographed dollars for the Tasting Room wall. Here's to you, Prager Family! Cheers!

Our Recipes

Grandma Betty's Avgolemeno Soup

- 40 oz chicken broth (make your own stock, if you want)
- 1 cup orzo
- 2 eggs
- ½ cup lemon juice (about 2 lemons)

Let stock come to boil. Add orzo and cook for ~8 minutes. Set aside.

Beat 2 eggs well in bowl. Add lemon juice and mix well.

Slowly integrate (temper) the egg mixture by pouring in a small amount of the stock. Keep stirring while you do this (no scrambled eggs allowed), and continue pouring and mixing until about ½ of the stock is in the egg mixture.

Transfer entire mixture back to the Orzo/stock pot. Stir well. Salt & pepper to taste. Eat & enjoy!

Crawfish & Andouille Sausage Gumbo

A true gumbo uses whatever you have around in the kitchen. Don't worry about being precise, just have fun.

- 2 green peppers
- 2 medium onions
- 2 stalks celery
- 2-4 cloves garlic
- 12 oz. chopped okra, fresh or frozen
- 40 oz. chicken stock
- 1 – 28oz. can crushed tomatoes
- ½ teaspoon cayenne (more to taste)
- Pinch of salt
- 1 teaspoon thyme
- 2 bay leaves
- ½ cup red wine
- ½ cup vegetable oil
- ½ cup flour
- ¼ cup red wine vinegar
- 1 lb. crawfish
- 1 lb. chopped andouille sausage
- 1 lb. sliced fresh mushrooms
- File powder (optional)
- Hot sauce (optional)

Chop peppers, onions, celery, and slice the garlic. Set aside in a bowl. In another bowl, chop up (1/4") the okra. If you're using fresh, you may want to wipe them down with a damp cloth first.

Combine stock, tomatoes, cayenne, salt, thyme bay leaves, and red wine into a large stock pan. Heat until it comes to a boil, then lower (or turn off). Set aside.

A good roux takes time. So pour a glass of your favorite wine, and place it by the stove, you're going to be there for a while. Your favorite beer works as well.

Heat a pan (cast iron when possible) over low heat for a few minutes with the oil. Add the flour, and start stirring. Keep stirring. Have some wine, and don't stop stirring. The reason for this is to make sure the roux doesn't burn. Don't stop stirring. Cook until it smells nutty and turns a dark, chocolaty-brown color.

Once the roux is ready, stir in the chopped vegetables. After 2 minutes, mix in the okra, cooking 10-15 minutes over low heat. Add the veggies to the stock mixture.

Pour in ¼ cup (or more, if you like your gumbo tart) red wine vinegar at this time, and cook over low heat for at least an hour.

Next, add the mushrooms and sausage, and continue to cook over low heat for another hour.

Finally, add the crawfish after the hour. They'll only need a few minutes to cook.

Taste, re-season if necessary, and serve over rice. For added flavor, sprinkle file powder atop the dish, and add your favorite hot sauce if you like it spicier.

Ya think it tastes good now? Wait 'til tomorrow, it tastes even better!

Mom's Pastitsio

- 1 onion, chopped
- 2 ½ lbs. chopped meat
- Seasonings for meat – allspice, cinnamon
- 2 cups tomato sauce
- 1 lb. ziti
- ¾ lb. butter
- Grated cheese (Parmesan)
- Eggs (1 whole, 2 egg whites, 2 egg yolks)
- 3 cups milk
- 3 tablespoons flour
- Bread crumbs

Saute onion in butter for a few minutes, then add chopped meat and seasonings (to taste). Also add tomato sauce. Cook until the chopped meat is browned, then remove from fire.

Boil ziti in salted water. Drain, then add ¼ lb. butter, grated cheese and 1 whole egg and 2 egg whites to ziti. Mix together.

To make béchamel sauce (what Mom called Crema), you need a double boiler (a bowl on top of a saucepan – it diffuses the heat. The bottom pan has boiling water.) Scald milk, and add 1/8 lb. butter and mix with flour to creamy consistency. Add salt and some grated cheese (to taste). Beat 2 egg yolks in bowl. Add béchamel/crema to egg yolks slowly, so that eggs don't scramble.

Grease 11"x16" pan with butter. Layer bottom of pan with bread crumbs. Then place a layer of ziti (Mom used to make sure all of the pasta was facing the same direction). Next, pour on all of the chopped meat mixture, followed by a final layer of lined-up ziti. Sprinkle a layer of cheese atop this. Finally, pour the béchamel/crema on top. Bake about ½ hour at 375°.

Bayside Bunnie's Brisket O' Beef

- 1 3-4 lb. Brisket
- 1 bottle of Heinz' Chili Sauce
- 1 package of Lipton Onion Soup mix
- 1 can of Pepsi (no Coke)

Mix the chili sauce, onion soup mix and can of Pepsi. Pour over brisket. Cook long and slow. Try it at 325° for at least 2 hours. If you want to cook it at a lower temperature (225°) for a longer amount of time, that's fine. When is it done? When it's "fork tender."

Feeding Others

So, you've had a fantastic meal. Perhaps you just dined at a four star restaurant. Maybe it was at a local or national event. You feel content and satisfied. However, did you ever think what happens to the tons of food prepared (yet never served)?

Websites to end hunger are prevalent, and it's wonderful to see that there are hundreds of local organizations whose mission is to end hunger in that community. Do a search on terms such as end hunger, and you'll find a large number of places doing great work.

The food community (including many chefs) also does yeoman's work to help bring food over to those who need it most. Many chefs keep a very low profile when doing so, not wanting attention…only wanting to do what's right. Thanks to all of you those folks doing the job to end hunger.

We've been fortunate to have worked with one such organization over the years, and are thrilled to share them with you.

CHARITY

TRUCKIN' THE FOOD AWAY

Rock and Wrap It Up
eliminate hunger in our lifetime
www.rockandwrapitup.org

There are great people you feel fortunate to have met in your lifetime. Syd Mandelbaum is on that very short list. Scientist, humanitarian (and lover of the Grateful Dead), Syd has made his mission in life to eradicate hunger. In 1991, he connected with music promoters and bands performing at New York's Jones Beach Theater to have them donate the backstage food excess to provide meals to local soup kitchens and shelters. By getting the bands to add riders to their contracts, Rock and Wrap It Up was able to ensure that the leftovers were delivered (that same night) to the shelters that need the food. In subsequent years, these riders have become more and more common, not only at this venue, but many around the country.

Check out Syd's blog (http://rockandwrapitup.blogspot.com), you'll learn more about his Hunger Manifesto. His goal is to create a world which feeds all who hunger, and eventually eliminate poverty.

Over the past 15 years, he and his wife Diane have reached out beyond concerts, mobilizing the volunteer organization to work with schools (College Wrap), sports teams (Sports Wrap) and even mayors of various cities to provide food to those who need it. Go to the website to learn more about these programs, and see how you (and your kids) can volunteer to help deliver food to those in need. Thank you, Syd and Diane.

Index

Jim & Peter's Top O' The 9s

Peter's 9 Favorite Eateries

#1 -The French Laundry, Yountville, CA

Jim and I were blown away with every exquisite taste, texture and flavor. After the meal, Chef Thomas Keller invited us into the kitchen just to meet us. We were stunned. We loved his food so much, and he wanted to thank *us* for enjoying it so. The meal of a lifetime.

#2 - Oggi, New York, NY

Sister to the famous Il Vagabondo; the first place I ever tasted osso bucco. Wow.

#3 - Delmonico's, Las Vegas, NV

Dinner, service, vino, style. My only meal in Vegas if I had to choose just one. Thank you Scott Farber.

#4 - Papaya King, 86th and 3rd, NYC

The best grilled franks, ever, with deli mustard & onions. Don't forget to wash it down with that one of a kind Papaya drink. Ah, the old neighborhood!

#5 - Nepenthe, Big Sur, CA

Each time I go there to eat and bask in that view, I wonder why I ever leave.

#6 - Harraseeket Lunch and Lobster, Freeport, ME

One minute in the briny, next minute in melted butter! Must eat corn on the cob.

#7 - Mother's Restaurant, New Orleans, LA

If I had but one sandwich left to eat in my life, it would be the Debris from Mother's, roast beef which falls into the gravy while baking in the oven. Did I mention Jerry's jambalaya?

#8 - Farallon, San Francisco, CA

The wine pairing with chef's menu is fresh, flavorful and fantastic. Ask Jim.

#9 - Spellos/Messinger Abode, Queens, NY

My brother's kitchen. If I'm there, I know I'm home.

Jim's Top 9 Memorable Meals

#1 - French Laundry, Yountville, CA

Have been fortunate enough to eat there twice…and looking forward to future dining experiences. Chef Keller says that after more than a few bites of anything, people have fully experienced the food. If/when you go there, do the tasting menu, and leave your choices in the hands of one of this country's greatest chefs.

#2 - Babbo, New York, NY

Another tough reservation to get, but soooo worth it (as with all good chefs, you can't go wrong at any of Mario Batali's places). If you eat there, try the Scottaditi (tiny lamb chops), or my wife's fave, the Mint Love Letters (small stuffed raviolis).

#3 Commander's Palace, New Orleans, LA

Doesn't matter who the chef is when you go there (it has been the training ground for Paul Prudhomme and Emeril Lagasse), the meal is always incredible, and the service sublime. It has re-opened for business!

#4 - Topolabombo, Chicago, IL

You haven't had great Mexican (in this country) unless you've eaten in one of Rick Bayless's restaurants. Food & service both out of this world, and, needless to say, an awesome tequila selection.

#5 - Delmonico's, Las Vegas, NV

Emeril's Las Vegas steakhouse. This one makes the list from both an amazing dinner with my brother for his 50th birthday, as well as their overall great service (including having one of the most indescribable wines I've ever had…so much so, I can't even describe it here, but I know Peter remembers it).

#6 - Mrs. Wilkes, Savannah, GA

Family-style, serving southern comfort food. Worth the trip to Savannah for this experience. Be prepared to wait on line to get in (single seating), and sit with people you've never met (but who are there for the food as well). Oh yeah, lunch will set you back a whopping $13. Bring cash, and remember you're going to need to bring your dishes back to the kitchen when you're done.

#7 - Al's, St. Louis, MO

When in St. Louis, this is my favorite restaurant, and has been for over 20 years (however, don't bypass

Tony's either). Steakhouse, great seafood, and service staff that seems to have been there forever.

#8 - Emeril's, New Orleans, LA

I know, he's on here twice. But the first time we went (early 90's..before he was EMERIL!), we were blown away. Met the chef through mutual friends, and we'll never forget that he sent to the table every dessert on his menu. Take a bite…pass to the right. Not sure which was my fave, between the Goat Cheese Cheesecake or the Banana Cream Pie. Or what about the… Such decisions!

#9 - Elias' Corner, Queens, NY

I could have put any number of family relatives' places at the top of a Greek cooking listing, but this small seafood restaurant in Astoria, Queens always delivers top quality fresh whole seafood, grilled to perfection. No frills…just awesome food.

The Fabulous Spellos Brothers

your guides to the 99s - The Best of the Web

coming in 2007

99 Music Lovers Websites You Can't Listen Without

99 Showbiz Websites You Can't Be A Star Without

99 Sports Fans' Websites You Can't Score Without

(You didn't think we'd leave page 99 blank, did you?)

www.the99s.com

www.ingramcontent.com/pod-product-compliance
Lightning Source LLC
Chambersburg PA
CBHW021240090426
42740CB00006B/619

* 9 7 8 0 6 1 5 1 3 6 1 2 7 *